Whisper in the Woods celebrates the beauty and value of Nature by sharing a carefully selected showcase of art, photography and literature. Each issue offers new ways for all of us to *Discover, Explore* and *Appreciate* the natural world we cherish.

Editor/Publisher
Kimberli A. Bindschatel

Founding Designer
Suzanne Conant

Illustrator
Rod Lawrence

Inspiration
Mother Nature

Associate Editor
Denise Baker
Pam McCormick

Contributors

Steve Brimm
Robert Domm
Mark Graf
Tom Haxby
Linda Henderson
Rich Kelly
Cindy Mead
Mike Moats
Bruce Montange
Stacy Niedzwiecki
Dean Pennala
Steve Petrides
Carl J. Ray
Brad Reed
Carl R. Sams II

Webmaster
Stacy Niedzwiecki

Journal Dogs
Kloe & Tucker

Special Thanks
Ken Bindschatel
Patrick Cannon
Suzanne Conant
Dewitt Jones

Cover Photograph
Kimberli A. Bindschatel

Printed in the U.S.A.
Progress Printers
Traverse City, MI

Volume Six, No. Three

To Subscribe:
For current rates, please visit
www.WhisperintheWoods.com
or write to:
Whisper in the Woods Subscriptions
P.O. Box 1014
Traverse City, MI 49685
(866) 943-0153

Change of Address:
The post office will not automatically
forward *Whisper in the Woods* when you
move. To ensure continuous service,
please notify us at least six weeks
before moving. Send your new address
and subscription number to: *Whisper
in the Woods* Subscriptions, P.O. Box
1014, Traverse City, MI 49685.

Submitting art, photography or writing:
Please download our guidelines at
www.WhisperintheWoods.com

We are proud to be affiliated with:
Kalamazoo Nature Center
Kalamazoo, Michigan
www.naturecenter.org

Chippewa Nature Center
Midland, Michigan
www.chippewanaturecenter.org

Ad Sales:
Toll-Free (866) 943-0153
ads@whisperinthewoods.com

Whisper in the Woods®
(ISSN 1543-8821) is published quarterly
by Turning Leaf Productions, LLC. We
strive for accuracy in the articles and hon-
esty in advertising. We reserve the right to
refuse any advertising that is inappropri-
ate or not in harmony with the editorial
policy. Please obtain written permis-
sion before reproducing any part of this
publication. ©2007 All rights reserved.
Registered trademark.

Member, International Regional
Magazine Association

About this issue: (ISBN 978-0-9785820-5-0) Issued Autumn 2007

In this issue, we celebrate five years of bringing the beauty of nature to
you! Thanks for your support and shared love of all that we cherish.

~Kimberli Bindschatel, Editor in Chief

Five years!
my thoughts...

Kimberli A. Bindschatel
Kimberli A. Bindschatel
Editor in Chief

I love Nature. Regardless of the weather–rain or shine–I see beauty. I love the smell when it rains. I love the feel of soft moss. I love the sound of wind in the leaves.

What I enjoy most about spending time in Nature is that I find solace and simplicity. I see Mother Nature as a great sage who pours forth wisdom in everything we experience. I learn something everywhere I look, whether it is conspicuous or veiled in metaphor. It's a joy to seek what nature can teach.

Before I started *Whisper in the Woods*, I was not feeling very positive about myself and my career. I felt that I needed to change. In retrospect, I think I was searching for a purpose. I had this nagging voice, from somewhere within, telling me things just weren't right. It is difficult to describe, like a gut feeling, but yet with a distinct message, "you're not on the right path." At first it was just a whisper, so faint it was unrecognizable. The more time I spent with Nature, the louder that voice seemed to become and before long it was strikingly clear. It was no longer a voice that I *heard*, it was *me* telling everyone "see how beautiful the world is!"

I had found my purpose: to share with others the beauty of Nature and the solace they can experience. I wanted to bring to others that feeling, that connection that I have with Nature. I wanted to encourage others to go out and appreciate Nature the way I do.

Whisper in the Woods started with this simple idea, a thought really, and from that point on, my entire life's perspective has changed dramatically. The mission of *Whisper in the Woods* became my passion, an overwhelming desire that fueled my efforts.

That single vision has sustained me through the good times and the bad. It has been an incredible journey that has given me so much. Most importantly, it has given me the life I was meant to live.

The greatest lesson I've learned in the last five years is that I didn't really need to change at all. I just needed to find a way to reveal the potential within myself that was dormant all along. Nature taught me that and now I see life's lessons in Nature everywhere I look.

When leaves turn beautiful reds, oranges and yellows in autumn, they don't really change. The green of summer simply fades away to reveal the brilliant color that was there all along. We all tend to put out an exterior self–what we allow others to see. If we just let that go and reveal our true selves, our beauty can shine through. Seasonal change is not only inevitable it is absolutely necessary. Nature embraces change. If we don't have snow, we wouldn't have spring melt to nourish the plants and fill streams with clean water. We should learn from past experiences, they nourish our life.

For me, it all stems from one defining moment. It was the middle of the night–you know that time when you are half asleep and half awake. I was tossing and turning, trying to come up with the right title, then it came to me like lightning.

WHISPER IN THE WOODS.

It was perfect. I sat right up in bed and shouted, "I've got it!"

WHISPER IN THE WOODS.

That title speaks to me. It speaks of respect. It embodies the essence of what one can experience by being quiet in the woods and simply listening. I kept saying it over in my mind,

WHISPER IN THE WOODS.

And I knew that I had found *my* voice.

Five Year Commemorative

Red-spotted Butterfly, ©Kimberli A. Bindschatel

Spring

We dance a joyous frolic upon the sun's return. We are intoxicated with the rich, moist scent of Earth and the perfume of blooms. Wildflowers grace the contours of the Earth's curves and trumpet spring's return. We welcome animal friends as they awaken from their deep winter slumber or return to their summer breeding grounds after a long journey. We become giddy with the promise of morels and asparagus. Our spirits nearly burst with the visual delight of zingy green trees, brilliant blue sky, bright white clouds and happy yellow sun.

Rod Lawrence

Tiny Star
©Carl R. Sams II carlsams.com

Green Frog and Duckweed
©Mark Graf grafphoto.com

Showy Lady Slipper, ©Rich Kelly

Blooms

Emerging Fern
©Mike Moats tinylandscapes.com

Fox in Daisies, ©Carl R. Sams II carlsams.com

American Copper Butterfly, ©Stacy Niedzwiecki stacyn.com

Trillium, ©Dean Pennala pennalaphotography.com

Green Dragonfly, ©Dean Pennala pennalaphotography.com

Pictured Rocks Spray Falls, ©Dean Pennala pennalaphotography.com

Young Raccoon, ©Mark Graf grafphoto.com

Summer

We bask in the long, lazy days of summer, warmed to the bone by generous sunshine. We dive into the cold, clear freshwaters of the Great Lakes to exhilarate our spirits. The long days entice us to explore the Earth at leisure. The Earth is bursting with voluptuous fertility; hillsides are thick with green growth, fruit swells, and fledglings come of age. Everything celebrates this season of ease and plentitude: butterflies flutter, flowers dance and trees sway in the breeze. Sunset over the lake beckons our contemplative gaze.

Sandhill Crane, ©Mark Graf grafphoto.com

Textures

Monarch on Goldenrod
©Linda Henderson

Fern On Stump, ©Mike Moats tinylandscapes.com

Dune Ridge
©Steve Petrides
naturephotosonline.com

Impressions
©Brad Reed
toddandbradreed.com

Ripples

Sunset, ©Cindy Mead northwoodsong.com

Water

Contemplation
©Carl J. Ray
carlray.smugmug.com

Common Loon, ©Bruce Montagne whisperwood.net

Stoney Beach, ©Tom Haxby tomhaxbyphotos.com

Elements

Chipmunk in Burrow, ©Cindy Mead
northwoodsong.com

Pines and Fog, ©Mark Graf grafphoto.com

Autrain Cascade, ©Dean Pennala pennalaphotography.com

Birch Bark Detail
©Steve Petrides
naturephotosonline.com

Great Horned Owl, ©Stacy Niedzwiecki stacyn.com

Autumn

Salmon burst upriver to spawn, pregnant fruit drops from trees, and the comforting scent of spiced leaves wafts on the breeze. The air's chill renders us more contemplative. Bright orange maple leaves against a brilliant blue sky threaten to set our eyes ablaze.

Rod Lawrence

Holy Water, ©Brad Reed toddandbradreed.com

Milkweed Seeds in Dew
©Mike Moats
tinylandscapes.com

Sunset

Frosted Maple Leaves, ©Dean Pennala pennalaphotography.com

Great Sand Bay, ©Steve Brimm brimmages.com

Hide & Seek
©Carl R. Sams II
carlsams.com

Dragonfly On Coneflower, ©Mike Moats tinylandscapes.com

Seeds

Muskrat in Pond, ©Mark Graf grafphoto.com

Cattails, ©Cindy Mead northwoodsong.com

Milkweed Buck, ©Carl R. Sams II carlsams.com

Autumn Burst of Color, ©Rich Kelly

Peace, ©Mike Moats tinylandscapes.com

Leaves

Wolf in Autumn Color, ©Rich Kelly

Sugar Maple in Autumn, ©Robert W. Domm rdommphoto.com

Winter

The first snow is like an old friend returning in this most sacred and introspective of seasons. The quilt of quiet snow reflects the periwinkle of dawn and dusk, and long slabs of cornflower blue tree shadows. Stars chime in the stark solitude of dark nights. We discover a newly sculpted landscape while ice fishing, snowshoeing and cross-country skiing. We luxuriate in snuggling with *Whisper in the Woods* by the fire with a steaming mug of rich hot chocolate.

Rod Lawrence

Birch in Snow, ©Steve Brimm brimmages.com

Ice on Lake St. Clair, ©Mark Graf grafphoto.com

Frozen

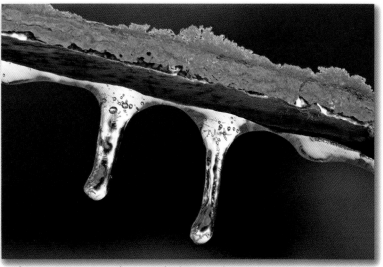

Iced Twig, ©Dean Pennala pennalaphotography.com

First Snow
©Carl R. Sams II
carlsams.com

Crystals

Seed Pods and Snow Mounds, ©Mark Graf grafphoto.com

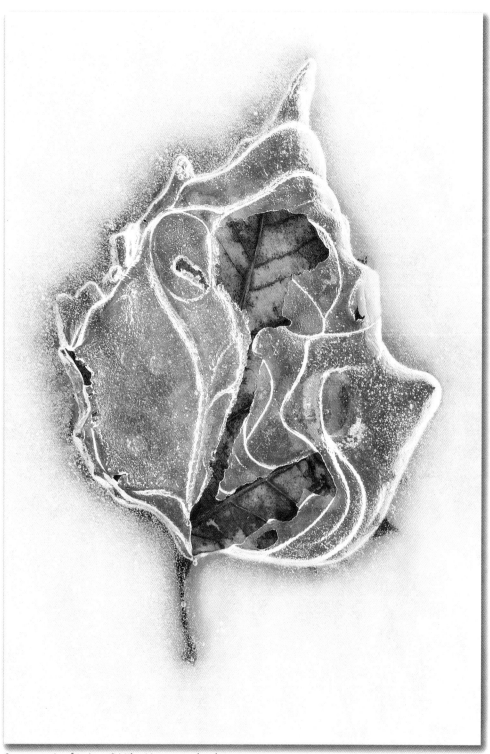

Sycamore Leaf in Ice, ©Mike Moats tinylandscapes.com

Red Pine and Hoar Frost, ©Steve Brimm brimmages.com

Snow

Acorns in Snow
©Mike Moats
tinylandscapes.com

Sculpted Snow on Lake Superior, ©Bruce Montagne whisperwood.net

Lone Ice Block, Lake St. Clair, ©Mark Graf grafphoto.com

Winter Sky Over Northern Lake Huron, ©Linda Henderson

Blue Skies

enjoy*Nature*.org

Destinations
nature travel destinations to explore in the Great Lakes region, whether you're hiking, paddling or cycling

Calender of Events
plan your outings, from moonlit hikes to cross-country skiing to artist appearances

Seasonal Watch
when and where to find Nature in her finest splendor, from spring wildflower blooms to peak autumn color, let fellow nature lovers know on our blog

Activities
Kids Treehouse, crafts and fun activities, Geocaching destinations

Marketplace
product reviews, from snowshoes to kayaks to backpacks as well as items to purchase

Galleries
post your own photographs, essays and poetry, or browse our featured artist galleries

E-Newsletter
sign up, it's free

Free E-Postcards
send beautiful images to your friends

... your path to nature!

www.enjoyNature.org

Brought to you by *Whisper in the Woods* in partnership with the Great Lakes Nature Alliance

Complete Your Collection Today!

Life in a Pond
Volume 5 No. 2

Gazing beneath the surface we discover our muse, intimations of our ancestors, the roots of our legends, and reflections of ourselves–and that the surface is but an illusion

Wolves of Isle Royale
Volume 5 No. 3

As messengers of the spirit world, wolves echo our untamed inner instincts, conjure the moon and offer equanimity with their dignity, grace and beauty

Snowshoe Trekking
Volume 5 No. 4

The solitude of snowshoes atop a sparkling quilt of shadows spilled in soothing hues deepens our perception, transforming the familiar to the new

The Healing Power of Nature
Volume 6 No. 1

Water's sparkling trickle soothes our troubles, fresh air restores our every particle, soft earth absorbs our cares, forests offer patient wisdom–Nature's caress is our ultimate healer

The Gift of Nature

Discover • Explore • Appreciate

Whisper in the Woods

Discover • Explore • Appreciate

Whisper in the Woods
Nature Journal

Summer 2006

Life in a Pond

As a gift for your family or friends, or even as a gift to yourself, *Whisper in the Woods* is a promise of quiet sunrises and gentle breezes.

Subscribers will enjoy the added benefit of receiving a collector's art print yearly.

Call Toll-Free
to Subscribe
(866) 943-0153
Subscribe online
www.WhisperintheWoods.com